Fishin' With

a

Mission

A Narrative of Fishing and Faith

By Professional Angler
Daryl Christensen

Fishin' With a Mission

A Narrative of Fishing and Faith

By Professional Angler
Daryl Christensen

A Christian Voice Publishing

ISBN: 0-9786580-8-6

Cover Design
Amy Poster

Editor
Ray Anderson

Graphic Design
Nick Furey

Publisher
A Christian Voice Publishing
102 S. 29th Ave West
Suite 103
Duluth, MN 55806

Acknowledgements

As with any book, the list of those who have in some way been a part of this one is long and their involvement varied. Yet without each of them, you probably wouldn't be reading this right now.

I have to start with my wife, Sherry, who gently prodded, encouraged, and prayed, knowing that once I finally got started, I would bring this work to completion.

My tournament sponsors over the past 20 years. Without their financial support most of the experiences in this book would never have occurred.

Professional walleye champion, Tommy Skarlis, who believed in my ministry and generously supported the publishing of this book with his finances.

My wife's friend and prayer partner, Tobi Bertzyk whose prayers for me and generosity were a big part in getting this narrative to print.

My spiritual mentors and advisors, Todd Forrest and Sam Timm for their direction, their prayers and their wisdom.

My dad and grandfather for taking the time to take me fishing.

About the Author

The son of an accomplished fly fisherman and grandson of a lifelong baitshop owner, Daryl Christensen grew up on the Fox River in Montello, WI where he honed his skills as a fisherman at an early age. By the time he was 10-years old, he was guiding anglers for bass, walleyes, catfish and panfish from his grandfather's baitshop while learning the art of fly-fishing for trout in area streams from his father.

From those humble beginnings more than 50 years ago, Christensen has become known as one of the top walleye anglers in North America today. In outdoor writer's circles, he is known as the "go-to-guy" when it comes to quotes on shallow water walleye fishing as well as breaking old myths about catching walleyes.

In-Fisherman Magazine has nicknamed him the "Jigmeister" for his expertise on jigging livebait as well as his breakthrough techniques for catching walleyes on jigging spoons.

His expertise is quoted extensively in books, videos, print and electronic mediums on an annual basis.

An accomplished writer himself, he has published more than 1,000 articles on the outdoors and fishing over the past four decades in publications across the country.

He has also written two books on walleye fishing and one on bass fishing and is the featured angler on the top-selling video, "Jigging Walleyes A to Z". He is also featured and quoted extensively in "Walleye Tactics, Tips & Tales" published by the North American Fishing Club.

As a speaker, he has appeared at almost every major sportshow across the country in more than 100 cities in 20 states and three Canadian provinces where he has shared his fishing knowledge with hundreds of thousands of anglers.

He has also proven his versatility as an angler by winning the prestigious Professional Walleye Trail Super Pro Championship Tournament in Lake Stockton, Missouri by casting jigs then following up with a first place finish at the PWT mid-western pro-am at Lake Erie while trolling crankbaits for suspended fish.

Today, at age 57, Christensen continues to be one of the top anglers on the In-Fisherman Professional Walleye Trail, where he has served for years on the circuit's advisory council. During his off season, he keeps busy speaking at clubs, boat shows and banquets across the country, giving more than 100 seminars on fishing and faith in 2005-2006.

He still lives near the Fox River in Montello with his wife of 36 years, Sherry. They have five grown children and 10 grandchildren.

Table of Contents

Chapter One

"A Mountain of Fish"

Have you ever been on a fishing trip in the mountains? I have a couple of times and I can tell you that there is something special about catching rainbow, golden and cutthroat trout from icy streams formed by melting glaciers. All around you are gigantic, snow-capped peaks with bighorn sheep, mountain goats, elk and bears as your only companions.

Between these lofty spires are valleys dotted with alpine meadows that are so lush and green that their contrast to the gray peaks can only be described as breath-taking. Birds of all kinds flourish in these meadows and the nearby forests, their songs ringing and echoing off the mountainsides in the cool of the day.

In late summer, the meadows are a splash of purple, yellow, red, blue, white and green as lupine, beargrass, Indian paintbrush and other flowers are in full bloom. Huckleberries and raspberries add to the color as they ripen in the warm, mid-day sun, much to the delight of birds and bears and of course, this fisherman.

Rockslides and avalanches have created homes for chipmunks and pikas who busy themselves collecting leaves and seeds to store in their burrows for the almost eight months of winter. I always marvel at how those little critters can live in such a brutal winter environment.

The slides have also created a score of tiny lakes, some of them more than 100 feet deep as millions of tons of rock and dirt slid into the mountain creek at various intervals through the steep pass. Below these lakes are magnificent waterfalls and cascades as the undaunted stream makes its way thousands of feet down into the foothills.

It is in these lakes that the cutthroats and rainbows live, their presence only revealed as they dimple the water's surface for hatching insects. Below the lakes where the rapids and falls tumble over boulders the size of army tanks is where you find the golden and brook trout, taking refuge in the smallest of eddies behind the massive rocks.

Since mink and kingfishers are the only other fishermen in the mountains, these fish seldom, if ever, see a fish hook, making them easy to catch on just about any fly that is presented to them. For me, fishing these unwary trout is great therapy after a tough couple of months on the tournament trail where the fish never seem so eager to be caught.

At night, there is nothing like the quiet of a mountain. It is amazing that something so awesome can make no sound; a stark contrast to the machines made by man or the cities where they live. No hum of airplanes or honking horns will be found there. No dirt bikes, no outboard motors, no people shouting. No sound at all except for the wind singing through the trees.

Some people go the mountains to "find themselves". Others go there to lose themselves. While hunting elk in the Bighorn Mountains many years ago, I had a hunting friend tell me that "we are as close to heaven as we'll ever get!" I'm glad that he was wrong on that account.

In many religious writings, mountains are often talked about as places of retreat for the prophets. Elijah, Moses, David and others often fled to the mountains to escape their pursuers. The 10 commandments were given on a mountain; Moses met God at the burning bush on a mountain and of course, Noah's boat rested on a mountain.

Jesus was always going to the Mount of Olives to pray and in fact, he went there just before his arrest and crucifixion. He also went there when he grew weary, like the time he preached to and fed the 5,000. Luke 6:12 says that he went to a mountainside to pray all night before choosing his disciples. When Jesus was transfigured, he went to Mount Tabor.

The evidence is clear that Jesus and others retired to the quietness of mountains to be alone with the Father. It wasn't about climbing higher to feel closer to God. It was about getting away from all of the distractions in the foothills of life. It was about attitude not altitude.

One of the biggest problems Christians have today with praying and hearing from God is that they try to do it while cluttering their minds with the cares of this world and the never-ending noise around them. Jesus encouraged his disciples to rise up early and pray because that is the quietest time of the day.

You might say that "I am not a morning person." Well, Jesus also retired at night and prayed. For some people, that may be their quietest time of the day. For me, however, it is time to sleep! I do know that if I do not rise early for my devotions and start my day by doing other things, I never get back to praying that morning.

Quiet time with God is the most important thing you can do each day. Whether it is done on a mountain, on your deck, in the bedroom or in the bathroom, if you desire to hear from God, shut out the noise, then pray and listen for His still, small voice.

Chapter Two

"Shore Lunch"

There is a time-honored tradition that takes place on the shores and islands of hundreds of lakes every day throughout the summer. It is a place and time where anglers gather to feast on the fruits of their labors, share casual conversation and take a break from a morning of intense fishing. Without it, there seems to be a sense of incompleteness to a fishing trip in Canada or the Northern United States. It is called the "shore lunch".

A shore lunch is a quite simple affair. I've attended many in my years of fishing and I've also cooked quite a few. In most cases, it is set up by the local guide who takes a couple of his client's fish and heads to shore. While on shore, he starts a fire, fillets the fish, cuts them in chunks and places them in a pan of hot oil, frying them to a golden-brown. A couple of cans of baked beans are also either placed in a kettle or cooked right in the can over the hot coals. A loaf of homemade bread or biscuits will top off the menu.

The guide most often starts the shore lunch while the anglers are still out fishing, but once the aroma of the cooking reaches the anglers, they head to shore in a hurry. Once there, the fish and beans are dispatched in an instant, washed down by ice-cold water. When the last crumb is eaten, the guide cleans up and douses the fire, while the anglers turn to stories of the day's fishing or perhaps seasons past.

Joining them in conversation will be ravens, jays and magpies coming to clean up anything that may have been dropped in the sand. One time at a shore lunch in Manitoba, we even had a curious bear eyeballing us from a ways off (which is where you always want a curious bear to be) undoubtedly waiting for us to leave before investigating the site for leftovers. We agreed that he had probably done this many times before.

Talk around a campfire is quite different than the chatter that takes place with friends during a meal at a restaurant. It is quieter, usually more wholesome and certainly more philosophical. There is something about the quiet of the northwoods, the lake, the call of the loons, the presence of a bear, the flickering campfire and men doing what they love, at least for a short time, away from the clamor and busyness of the world.

I don't know when the shore lunch became popular, but I suspect it was simply a tradition brought here by European explorers who pretty much had shore lunch as part of their daily routine. Of course native people were doing shore lunch long before the first white man landed on North American shores.

Historically, I do know of one shore lunch that took place almost 2,000 years ago. It is recorded in the Bible in

John 21: "When they landed, they saw a fire of burning coals there with fish on it, and some bread. Jesus said to them, 'Bring some of the fish you have just caught'." Now if this doesn't sound like a fishing guide cooking shore lunch, I don't know what does!

After they had eaten the shore lunch, Jesus engaged the disciples in conversation. I'm sure they talked about the big catch of fish they just experienced, as well as how good the lunch tasted after fishing hard all night. But soon the conversation became much more profound as Jesus forgave Peter of his denial and reinstated him as His disciple. This all took place at a shore lunch on the Sea of Galilee.

The Savior of this world has a shore lunch waiting for you. In Revelation 3:20 he says: "Behold, I stand at the door and knock; if anyone hears My voice and opens the door, I will come in and eat with him, and he with me." Jesus says that He is the bread of life. Are you ready to join with Him at the shore lunch He has prepared for you? Are you ready to receive His free gift of eternal life?

If so, simply say these words: "Jesus, I need you in my life. Forgive me of the mess I've made. I receive you as my Lord and Savior. I receive your free gift of eternal life." Now, let's do lunch.

Chapter Three

"A Grizzly Reminder"

Fly fishing for trout is something that I really enjoy. There is something magical, almost mesmerizing about a dry fly drifting down the current into a deep hole of an icy-cold trout stream. When I am trout fishing, I can get lost in thought, forgetting about the cares of this world or maybe a poor performance in yesterday's tournament.

I also like to tie my own flies. I'm not all that good at it, though. My father and grandfather could take tiny pieces of thread, chenille, and feathers, put them on the tiniest hook and make the whole concoction look like a real midge or mayfly. My creations tend to look more like a bug on the windshield, but some trout still find them to their liking.

There are many trout streams within 15 minutes of where I live, but I always wanted to fly fish for trout in the glacial creeks of northern Montana. So a few years ago, I packed up my family and went west, stopping to fish several of the famous trout rivers in Montana and Wyoming. It was great medicine for me to get away from the intensity of tournament fishing for a couple of weeks and enjoy a relaxing fishing vacation.

When tournament fishing, I am constantly alert to every subtle change in weather, water temperature, fish movement, wind direction and so on. There is no time to relax and enjoy the day. There is simply too much at stake. But fly fishing is different. For me, wading in a stream and casting a fly is as relaxing as it gets. However, being a competitor at heart, I still want to catch some fish.

One day, while fishing a small stream in Glacier Park, I was catching brook trout on almost every cast. They were chunky fish and I thought a fish fry for my family and friends would be much appreciated. I caught and released trout after trout, keeping several during three short hours of fishing.

The day was also gorgeous with only a slight breeze blowing and the only sounds were those of the birds singing from the thick willows that bordered the creek on both sides and the creek itself, bubbling over glacial rocks. I felt like I was the only person on earth, lost in time and space, wallowing in the pure pleasure of being in God's great outdoors and catching the prettiest brook trout I had ever seen.

Suddenly, it all changed. The light, cool breeze was stilled. The birds ceased singing. Something wasn't right. I felt the hair stand up on the back of my neck as I glanced both ways up and down the creek; nothing. But I knew, instinctively, that something wasn't right. A lifetime in the outdoors tells a person these things.

I slowly made my way around the next bend in the river and there in the mud along the sandbar was a grizzly track. It was easily a foot long and so fresh that water was still seeping into the track. And here was I, smelling like a 160 pound brook trout. It was time to go. I eased my way back down the creek, climbed the hill and made it safely to a well-worn hiking trail back to camp. I was safe. The following year, two hikers were mauled by a grizzly at that same spot. I wonder if it was the same bear.

All of us have simple pleasures that we enjoy and there is nothing wrong with that. The danger comes, however, when we get so caught up in those pleasures that they can consume our every thought and too much of our time. Worse yet, they can lead us into sin and away from where God wants us to be. Pleasure isn't always sinful. After all, the Bible says that God takes pleasure in us. But it should always be kept in perspective.

That day on the stream I was so caught up in the pleasure of the day and catching fish, I failed to be alert to the present danger of roaming grizzly bears. In my case, I was still able to avoid an encounter. Some aren't so fortunate. In our physical life, we have been given a gift of instinct to warn us of danger. In our spiritual life, we have been given the gift of the Holy Spirit and discernment to warn us of spiritual dangers.

It is important that we use these gifts to keep the pleasures of this life from becoming a grizzly bear of sin that can destroy us.

Chapter Four

"Stay in the School"

Having logged tens of thousands of hours while fishing on lakes, rivers and streams across the North American Continent, I am constantly amazed at Creation's perfect order.

In spring, millions of birds migrate north just as insects begin to hatch, offering plenty of fuel for their long flights. Animals shed their warm winter coats so they can tolerate the hot days of summer. Fish begin to stir, moving into spawning areas, with almost every species spawning at a different water temperature so that spawning areas aren't over-crowded. Can you imagine bluegills spawning at the same time as northern pike? It would be an awful scary time for bluegills to be sure!

It seems like I learn or see something new almost every time I'm on the lake or stream, but one of the things that I find most interesting is when small baitfish gather in big circles and move as one seemingly single organism around the lake. You've probably seen this yourself, if not on the lake, then watching some nature show on television. It is simply fascinating to watch their synchronized movements through the water.

Scientists believe that these small fish do this to confuse predators, making themselves look like a huge ball-like animal, thus avoiding being eaten. If a predator does strike, the scattering of the minnows in every direction also is supposed to be confusing to a hungry gamefish.

There's been numerous times when I've seen this scenario played out. A big northern pike would cruise the shallows, coming onto a school of shiners. When the school is spotted, the pike power-surges into it, only to miss what looked like any easy meal. Once the pike passed through the school as the minnows exploded in every direction, it would be only a matter of seconds before they re-grouped into a big ball of baitfish. Sometimes the pike will hit the school two or three more times before giving up. Other times, it might actually catch one of the small baitfish.

As long as the school of minnows worked together as a unit and united quickly after scattering, the individuals were protected. They had strength and security in numbers. But woe to any minnow that lagged behind the school, or swam too far from the group: that's the one the pike could easily catch and eat.

As Christians, we can learn a valuable lesson from a school of tiny minnows. Hebrews 10:25 warns us to "not forsake the assembling of ourselves together" so that we might encourage one another. I know too many Christian fishermen and hunters who spend Sundays in a tree stand or in a boat and call it "their" church. These men are spiritually weak and vulnerable to the predator, Satan, because they lack accountability with other believers. I know, because that is how I feel when I miss church a couple of weeks in a row.

Like a voracious northern pike, our "enemy the devil prowls around like a roaring lion looking for someone to devour." (1 Peter 5:8). Seldom have I ever seen Satan wage an all-out attack on a strong group of Christians. But I often see him hard at work on those who have left the safety of the school (church body) to go it alone because of the world's temptations. In more cases than I care to count, he quickly devours them up.

As believers of "like and precious faith" we need to stay in the school.

It is safe there.

Chapter Five

"The Secret Spot"

Every fisherman has a secret spot. It's a special place they go to fish where they can almost always count on catching something no matter how tough the fishing might be on that particular day. Sometimes it is one spot out of dozens of "good spots"; other times it might be a secret spot on every lake, river or stream they fish. It is most often their favorite spot to fish as well.

Since I have the privilege to fish lakes and rivers all over North America, I am often asked which place is my favorite. That can be a tough question to answer since I have fished on so many wonderful lakes and rivers. I do have favorites, though; places that immediately come to mind.

One such place is Snow Creek on Fort Peck Reservoir in Montana. As you enter this "creek" which is a large, flooded ravine off the main lake, your breath is taken away by its beauty. Mule deer and elk are often seen while fishing there and the fishing is terrific. You seldom, if ever, see another angler. Even if the fishing was poor, Snow Creek would always be one of my favorites.

Then there is the mouth of the Little Sac River on Lake Stockton in Missouri. It's a small spot where I caught the fish that won me first place in the Walleye Super Pro tournament. How can that *not* be one of my favorite places to fish?

I can think of a dozen others, but hands down, my favorite secret fishing spot is on the Fox River where I live. I caught my first walleye there five decades ago and the spot still is a haven for these tasty fish. The spot itself is really no secret as other anglers are often seen fishing there, but there is a spot-on-the-spot that most aren't aware of and that is what makes this my favorite.

The spot is also where I spent many hours fishing with my dad as a youngster and where we fished together the last year of his life. It is a spot I have taken my own sons to fish and this past year, my grandsons and granddaughters. It doesn't matter if I take any fish home from this spot, because I always take home memories.

All of us need a spot like this, whether we fish or not. Jesus talks about such as spot in Matthew 6:6 because He understood the value of having a quiet, undisturbed place where we could meet with Him. Here is what He said: "But when you pray, go into your room, close the door and pray to your Father, who is unseen. Then your Father, who sees what is done in secret, will reward you."

Many people call such a place a "prayer closet", but it doesn't necessarily mean a closet. It can be any place that is quiet and secret, so that nothing can distract you from your time of prayer. It can be your bedroom, den, dining room table, car, picnic table or many other places where you go to talk with God.

For me, it is more of a time of day than place. I like to rise at 4:00 a.m.; which is normally a very quiet time of day. There is little in the way of distractions that early in the morning and is a perfect time for me to have fellowship with my Lord and Savior. At times, I might simply stay put in bed and spend time in prayer. Other times, I will get up and pray in the den or living room. No music, no radio, no tv, no other people walking around to distract me. Even the cat leaves me alone this early in the day!

Do you have a secret place? If not, it is time you did. I know how busy people are today and that many if not most Christians "pray on the fly". While it is good to pray at anytime and all times of the day, nothing can replace that half-hour or more of undisturbed intimacy with Christ.

Try it. You might be amazed how your relationship with God will grow and how that undisturbed time with Him at the start of the day will help dictate how the rest of the day will go.

Chapter Six

"A Way That Seems Right"

After 26 years of tournament fishing, I'm convinced more than ever that fishing is 90% mental and 10% skill. In fact, I think that the mental game in any sport is what separates success from failure most of the time. The decisions a quarterback makes, the shot or pass a basketball player makes, the pitch thrown by a pitcher, the club chosen by a golfer can all make or break their game.

In tournament fishing, as in other sports, most of the professionals are on a similar par when it comes to skill and equipment. Some may be better at a particular technique than others such as trolling, casting, live bait rigging or jigging. But by and large, most have mastered each of these various methods quite well. As a result, it is the professional who makes the best decisions during the competition days, and not necessarily the most skilled who often wins the tournament.

In tournament fishing, there are lots of decisions to be made such as: "Do I stay on this spot longer or move?" "Do I use this bait or that bait?" "Do I fish faster or slower?" "Do I make the 40-mile run or fish close and save time?" "Should I troll crankbaits, fish crawler harnesses, rig live bait, jig, Lindy rig, use bottom-bouncers, cast cranks, fish the weeds, fish the rocks, fish the flats, fish the open water, use 6, 8, 10, or 12-pound test, fish the windy side or calm side?" And the list goes on and on.

When I make the wrong decision I usually tell people I "zigged" when I should have "zagged". Of course, when I make the right decision I usually don't have to explain it because I had a high finish or won the event. Sometimes I am positive that I made the right move, only to have a disastrous finish. That's when it is easy to lay blame on other factors, but the bottom line is that when I saw that the decision I was making wasn't leading to victory, I needed to make a different decision to affect the outcome.

Proverbs 14:12 says: "There is a way that seems right to a man, but in the end leads to destruction." Although I can certainly apply that verse to my fishing decisions and the other decisions that I make throughout my life, I believe that that verse, more than any other, speaks about today's attitudes concerning eternal salvation.

How often do we hear people say: "I think there are many ways to God" or "I believe that everyone goes to Heaven no matter what they believe?" If this were true, than what was the point of Christ's death on the cross? If we can get to Heaven some other way, then He came and died for nothing.

In John 14:6, Jesus proclaimed: "I am the way, the truth and the life, no one comes to the Father but by me." It is clear from this statement about Himself, that the only way to Heaven was through Jesus. Again, it comes down to making the right decision. Many people will say that they will decide for themselves what they want to believe about God, about Jesus, about eternity. Yet the Lord has made it very clear what the right "Way" to eternal life should be.

Proverbs 3:5 states: "Trust in the Lord with all your heart and lean not on your own understanding". Since I've learned to trust in Him, I find that I am making much better decisions, even in fishing tournaments. But I still sometimes find myself following that "way that seems right to a man but in the end leads to destruction". In a fishing tournament, that can be fixed, but in eternity, the wrong decision can lead to eternal destruction.

Don't let yourself be deceived by the world view that there are many ways to God. Jesus has made it clear that there is only one way and that is through Him and the sacrifice He made on the cross for our mistakes. He did that so we could have eternal life. Make a decision for Christ today.

It is the Way that IS right to a man and in the end leads to eternal life!

Chapter Seven

"Trust Your GPS"

Modern technology has made great strides in almost every aspect of our lives today and that includes fishing. We have better boats, motors, rods, reels, electronics and other equipment today than even a few years ago. All of these tools help anglers catch more fish if they know how to use them properly. But for tournament anglers, fishing guides and many recreational anglers, the most important piece of equipment they carry is their "GPS" or Global Positioning System.

A GPS is nothing more than a very advanced, digital compass that helps anglers to navigate to a precise location entered into the unit prior to heading out onto the lake. It is so accurate that you can get within a few yards of a spot even if that spot is hundreds of miles from the launch site. Most GPS units can store more than 1,000 waypoints for future reference.

Today, ships, planes, buses and even many private automobiles are equipped with GPS units. Wildlife researchers, forest rangers and even botanists use GPS technology to locate and record specific coordinates for tracts of land or location of transmittered animals, birds and fish. Hunters use GPS as well to help them find their way to camp and out to specific hunting areas.

As a tournament angler and guide, I find the GPS to be the one tool on my boat that I trust the most. I know that it will take me to the spots I want to go, reducing the time I used to spend driving in circles while trying to triangulate objects on shore. But while that might be important, the real significance of the GPS is navigation and safety.

Quite often, especially on big bodies of water, fog can come in quickly. Even if I am 15 miles offshore, I can simply punch in the boat landing and the GPS will guide me through the fog straight to the landing. Without it, I would have been lost numerous times, (although I always have a compass for backup).

Many times during our tournament competition on the Great Lakes, boats that break down and anglers in the water can be quickly found simply by sending their GPS coordinates out to the Coast Guard or other anglers via marine band radio. Several lives have been saved thanks to the pinpoint accuracy of the GPS.

Today's GPS units also have maps of many of the lakes and show navigation hazards, buoy lines, channels and water depth. Once navigated through, the unit will record a plot trail so that the boater can easily re-trace his route without running aground if fog or darkness sets in. Because GPS technology works off of satellites and is unaffected by weather and terrain, it far and above the most accurate means of navigation we have today. But it isn't perfect.

Because GPS units are digital, they can be highly susceptible to water damage and jarring, both which are commonplace on boats. And if your battery goes dead, your GPS will also go dead. A spare battery will solve that problem. The most important thing, however, is that you have to trust what the GPS is telling you, especially in low visibility when your internal compass is convincing you that you are going in the wrong direction.

Do you know that God has given us a "GPS" to help us through our Christian lives? I like to call Him "God's Paraklete Spirit" (GPS) or the Holy Spirit. The Greek word, parakletos, means; "one called alongside to help," or counselor and guide. Like a digital GPS, the Holy Spirit guides us through the fogbanks and sometimes the darkness we encounter in our Christian lives.

In John 16:13, Jesus tells us "But when he, the Spirit of truth, comes, he will guide you into all truth." When we have God's "GPS" we have the promise that we will be guided in ALL truth. We will be given the gift of discernment as the Holy Spirit works in our lives and guides us in our daily navigation of this earth.

In John 14:16-17, Jesus said: "And I will ask the Father, and he will give you another Counselor to be with you forever- the Spirit of truth. The world cannot accept him, because it neither sees him nor knows him. But you know him, for he lives with you and will be in you." In John 25:26 Jesus continues: But the Counselor, the Holy Spirit, whom the Father will send in my name, will teach you all things, and will remind you of everything I have said to you."

In these verses, Jesus promises us that the GPS he sends us will live *in* us. The events of the world may jar us, our batteries might run down and someone might throw a bucket of cold water on your Christian walk today. But thank the Lord that he has given us an internal GPS that cannot be damaged, but continues to guide us in our daily lives.

Do you remember those days before you came to Christ? They were days filled with making bad choices, days of sin, days of disappointment, depression, disillusionment and sometimes despair. They were days of nowhere to go, nowhere to turn, no one to listen, no one who cared. There was no peace, a life of fear, a life of sin. In 1 Corinthians 2, the Apostle Paul describes those days in verses 14: "The man without the Spirit does not accept the things that come from the Spirit of God, for they are foolishness to him, and he cannot understand them, because they are spiritually discerned."

In that same chapter, in verses 10-13, Paul describes how we as Christians, with the Holy Spirit dwelling in us, can live a completely different life from that of the one described above. He says: "but God has revealed it to us by his Spirit. The Spirit searches all things, even the deep things of God. For who among men knows the thoughts of a man except the man's spirit within him? In the same way no one knows the thoughts of God except the Spirit of God.

We have not received the spirit of the world but the Spirit who is from God, that we may understand what God has freely given us. This is what we speak, not in words taught us by human wisdom but in words taught by the Spirit, expressing spiritual truths in spiritual words."

Guiding us through our daily Christian lives is only one of the many works of the Holy Spirit, yet without that guidance, we could easily become confused or lost. Sometimes Christians can become so caught up in the "gifts of the Spirit" that they forget about the counseling and guiding of the Spirit.

There is one other way that a digital GPS won't function. Simply hit the "off" button. When God's Paraklete Spirit speaks to you, giving you that little "check" in your heart, do you hit the "off" button? Or do you "listen to what the Spirit" is telling you. Do you follow the Spirit's lead, His guidance?

Do you trust your "GPS"?

Chapter Eight

"Peace Like a River"

Is there anything more peaceful than a slow drift down a lazy river on a warm summer's day? I don't believe so. There is something about the slow-moving current, the singing birds and the scent of flowers blooming along the riverbank that is mesmerizing to the soul.

There are days when I will take my kayak or canoe and enjoy a peaceful day on the river. On those days, I will leave my fishing gear behind because I don't want the distraction of trying to catch fish while enjoying the solace that the river has to offer.

Since it is a known fact that most men can only concentrate on one thing at a time, when I'm fishing, I rarely hear or feel what else is happening around me. Fishing also is an obsession with me. Yes, it is an obsession that I enjoy immensely but one that can keep me from enjoying the creation that's all around me.

You see, for me it is never about going fishing for relaxation. I fish for one purpose and that is to catch fish, otherwise why take a fishing pole? It's kind of like going bird watching and not seeing any birds. What would be the point? Maybe it's just a guy thing or something.

On the other hand, my wife can go fishing, not catch anything and say she really enjoyed the day. I've always wondered how she can do that. Of course, one of her favorite sayings is "When God gives you lemons, make lemonade". Personally, I've never cared much for lemonade or fishing and not catching fish.

Sometimes when I'm just walking, I'll leave my binoculars at home. Being an avid bird watcher, it is easy to forget the reason for my hike which is to be alone with God, and get caught up in looking at the birds around me. This is especially true during migration when the treetops are literally dripping with warblers and other birds.

Living the life of an outdoorsman means that there are days when I actually have to force myself to be peaceful, to be quiet; to wait on the Lord. The Bible talks a lot about peace. Jesus is called "The Prince of Peace". It also states that Christians have a "peace that passes all understanding". At least we are supposed to.

Sometimes, the waters aren't always calm even for Christians. As a tournament angler, I have fished in 10-12 foot waves on the Great Lakes. I can tell you that there is little peace to be found on such days, especially if storms roll in and I am 20 miles off shore. The waves will crash into the boat, often filling it with hundreds of gallons of water. It is unsettling indeed.

Storms in our lives can be the same way. I remember the day my father died. I had never felt such grief. Waves and waves of sorrow washed over me, drenching me in a sadness I had never experienced before or since. Yet, mixed with the sadness was the knowledge that he was at last home with his Savior and peace would fill my heart.

One of my favorite hymns is "It is Well with My Soul". The first verse sums up what the Word of God talks about when it tells us to have peace: *"When peace like a river attendeth my way, when sorrows like sea billows roll, whatever my lot thou has taught me to say, it is well, it is well with my soul".* I can seldom sing this verse without tears welling up in my eyes.

No matter what this world throws at us, peace or turmoil, we have the hope and promise of everlasting life in Christ. If you haven't experienced that kind of peace, why don't you ask Jesus to come into your life today?

Doing so would be well with your soul.

Chapter Nine

"Don't Take the Bait"

Part of my job as a professional fisherman is to travel around the country and give seminars at boat shows and fishing shows. I always like to wrap up these talks with a question and answer period. Quite often, someone will ask if our technology has taken the fun out of fishing or has made catching fish so easy that it has become "unfair chase". My reply usually is that the fish still have to take the bait.

There is no doubt that fishing has come a long way in the past 50 years, especially in the area of lures. If you've ever been to a fisherman's mega-mall like Bass Pro Shops or Gander Mountain, you know what I mean. Every kind of lure in every color imaginable can be found at these stores. And you know something? Almost all of them will catch fish when used at the right time under the right circumstances.

Years ago, my friends Ron and Al Lindner invented a simple formula to catch fish. It is still used by all professional anglers today. It was called Fish + Location + Presentation = Success or F+L+P=S. This is always the basic formula we use to catch fish in tournaments or fishing for fun.

First you decide what fish (F) you want to catch (then learn all you can about that species). Then you seek out a location (L) where the fish will be. Then you choose the proper lure with the correct Presentation (P) and you catch the fish (S).

Here's an example: Say I want to catch some largemouth bass, it is early spring and I am fishing on a reservoir. I know that bass in reservoirs will be in the shallows in spring because the water is warmer and the bait fish are there. I also know that they will be by any structure such as stumps, branches, old vegetation or docks. So I have the Location nailed down.

Because the bass are shallow, I know that they will be vulnerable to several lure presentations and that I will want to present the lure on or slightly below the surface. A spinnerbait would be my first choice because I can crank it slowly around almost any structure. If the water is clear and the day sunny, I would use white or chartreuse; if it's cloudy, I would go with black.

Fishing a spinnerbait is an aggressive presentation designed to trigger a quick response from a bass or pike. But sometimes they will just follow and not hit the bait. That is when a more subtle, tantalizing approach will work, such as twitching a plastic worm on the bottom or a floating stickbait on the surface.

I've probably caught more bass and won more tournaments with the finesse approach than I have with the more aggressive techniques. Both will work and sometimes the aggressive approach is necessary to trigger a strike or cover more water. Overall, I believe that a more subtle Presentation works the best.

Now that I have the FLP nailed down, I only have to go fishing and catch some fish to complete the equation.

When I first became a Christian, I thought about how the devil uses a similar formula to catch people in his snare. He studies us just as we study the fish we want to catch. He chooses the right time, lure and location, presents his temptation, and if we take the bait, it equals sin (S) which is success for him.

Does he tempt the businessman when he is home with his family? No, he waits until he is away from home, at a motel, when he is tired, late at night (Location). He chooses the right lure, such as an R- rated movie or perhaps an equally lonely business woman (Presentation). The man, like a fish after a lure, must decide whether to take the bait or resist the temptation.

Just as a professional angler knows a fish's weakness and vulnerability, so does Satan know right where to tempt the Christian. The Bible says to "resist the devil and he will flee". It reminds me of the many times when I'm trying to catch some fish and they just won't bite. What do I do? I leave that bunch of resistant fish and find another school that I can tempt into biting. That is exactly what Satan does when a Christian resists his presentations!

What lures and presentations has the devil used on you throughout your life, even yet today? Pray that the Lord will give you the strength to resist the devil's schemes. Pray each morning that His Holy Spirit will help you to keep alert. Pray for the person who is tempting you to gossip, to lust, to lie, to cheat, to criticize. The devil really hates it when you pray for the one he is using to tempt you.

Finally, try this: when you are facing temptation, pray for someone who needs Jesus in their life. THAT will really make the devil flee!

"Resist the devil and he will flee from you"
James 4:7b

Chapter Ten

"Christmas Memoirs"

Christmas can mean many things to different people and can invoke happy and sometimes painful memories, often at the same time. My dad was a great lover of Christmas. After his retirement, he carved and painted many different ethnic versions of St. Nick, selling them to local craft shops and tourist attractions. Sometimes he would go to the schools or library and tell stories about Christmas, his long white hair and beard adding to the effect of the season.

When I was a child, I can remember Dad working in our basement to make Christmas presents for his 7 children. He was laid off from construction that winter and money was scarce, but he was determined to make the day a happy one for his kids. A curious and often disobedient child, I would sneak a peek through the cracks in the floor, watching him as he painted a rocking horse he made for my little sister. Over in the corner, was a green and white sled that caught my eye. Dad sanded and re-painted the old sled and straightened out the steel runners. It had my name on it.

We still have Christmas at that house every year, but it is hard to get everyone there. Dad went home to be with the Lord a few years ago, but the memories of Christmas' past are still overpowering. We sing old hymns and tell Christmas stories so that our children and grandchildren can know what December 25th means to us as Believers.

In almost 60 years, I have only missed one Christmas at that house. It was in 1970 and I was in the Army in Camp Casey, Korea. I called home, allowing for the time difference so that I could talk to everyone there. The background laughter made me so homesick that after I hung up the phone, I walked to the local village, bought a new sweater from a storefront shop and gave it to one of the "business girls".

"Merry Christmas," I said, as I handed her the gift. To this day I will never forget her bewildered look as she took the sweater then walked with me back to the compound. My Korean wasn't the greatest as I attempted to explain to her that it was a gift and that in America, it was Christmas Eve and millions of people were giving gifts. She didn't seem to understand, but thanked me for the sweater just the same.

I wasn't serving God back then but today I wonder if that girl, who was probably 15 or so, might now have become a Christian through the huge revival that has taken place in that Asian nation over the past decade. In fact, South Korea sends out more Christian missionaries today than any other nation in the world. It makes me smile to think of the thousands of Korean missionaries explaining to people all over the world what Christmas means, just as I did to that poor girl 35 years ago.

Some folks feel sadness around Christmas, even though they are bombarded with joyful Christmas songs and people being friendlier to them than usual. I'm one of those people. But then again, I'm also one of those guys who can't sing two verses of *Amazing Grace* or *Great is Thy Faithfulness* without tears welling up in my eyes. I do my best to put on a cheerful face at Christmas and fight hard against the feelings of being melancholy. I think I mostly feel this way because, like my dad, I want Christmas to be every day or at least I want people to treat others like every day was Christmas.

I guess what makes me most sober around this time of year, is the fact that we are commemorating the birth of Jesus Christ. I love little babies and when I think of our Savior as that little baby, I am saddened that He had to be born to die for my sins. Yet at the same time, I am also thankful and filled with joy that I have been saved. It's that old feeling happy and sad at the same time thing, you know?

I also feel saddened by the way the birth of Christ has been commercialized and perverted all around the world. Too many people focus on receiving gifts instead of giving them. Most of the new "Holiday" movies are a mockery, with scripts that celebrate New Age and rarely, if ever, mention the word "Christmas". And Christmas parties are often nothing more than pagan feasts. I know; I used to go to a lot of them.

People often ask me if I can recall my best Christmas ever. Although I think every Christmas had happy times with the better ones being when I was a child, I find that question quite easy to answer. My best Christmas ever was in 1988. That's the year I gave my heart to Christ.

That's the year I realized what Christmas was truly all about.

Chapter Eleven

"Counting Fish!"

Don't you just love fishermen? I mean, who else can catch a five pound fish and have it grow to 10 pounds before you even get it home? Just about every bait and tackle shop has a sign that says: "All fishermen are liars except for me and you and I'm not so sure about you".

Through the centuries fishermen have gained a reputation for exaggeration both in the size of the fish they catch, but also in the number. I've witnessed this firsthand hundreds of times and can't help but smile at the excitement in an angler's voice as he tells his fishing tale.

Now, I'm not saying here that all fishermen are liars. I think, however, that they often suffer from memory lapses when it comes to the true size and number of fish they have caught (except for me and you and I'm not so sure about you).

Exaggerating one's catch is nothing new. In fact, when I look at the book of John, I often wonder about those fishermen in the story related in Chapter 21.

Here are seven of the eleven disciples out in Peter's boat fishing all night without catching anything. They see a man standing on shore and my guess is they assumed it was a local guy, because when he told them to cast their net on the other side of the boat, they did it without argument. Hey, if a local angler tells me to try a spot, I'm doing it!

We all know what happened next. They had such a great catch of big fish that they couldn't even lift the net into the boat. They had to drag the net behind the boat up to shore, then jump in the water and haul the net and fish in by hand.

Once on the shore, they counted the big catch because the Bible records that there were 153 fish in the net. Now I don't know about you, but I think it is pretty cool that Jesus would sit down and help them count their fish! You don't suppose He did that because He knew that the number would grow to huge proportions once seven different anglers related the story to their friends?

Remember, Simon Peter was known to be an impulsive and boastful man. Kind of like many fishermen I know (except for you and me and I'm still not so sure about you). After all, not too many days before, he had denied he even knew Christ on three different occasions.

But that day, on the shores of the Sea of Tiberias, around a campfire of burning coals and shore lunch, Jesus reinstated Peter as the head of His church, forgiving him of his denial.

Isn't that great? No matter what our latest lie was, Jesus is there to forgive all of us (including me and I AM sure about you)!

Now, let me tell you about the big walleye I caught the other day. You see, that fish was so huge that when I reached for it with the net, it.......................................

Chapter Twelve

"Tossed by the Wind"

Anyone who has ever done much fishing knows that wind, depending on its velocity, can be a blessing or a curse. Wave action can break up sunlight penetration as well as visibility, so that a fish cannot see an approaching angler or boat as well as it can when the lake is flat calm.

Waves crashing into a shoreline can stir up the bottom, making clear water turbid. Fish find this situation much to their liking, as baitfish become disoriented and easier to catch, since the minnows and small fish cannot see an approaching predator.

Walleye anglers especially like some wind for the above reasons, and refer to waves in the one to two foot range as a "walleye chop". In fact, some rely so heavily on the "chop" that they don't even go walleye fishing when the lake is flat calm.

Fishing in waves under two feet is pretty simple to an accomplished angler with the proper equipment for positioning a boat, but sometimes the waves can get so big that it not only becomes difficult to fish, but downright dangerous to even be on the water.

During my 30 years of tournament competition, I have been in every wind situation imaginable. I can recall hugging a bluff along Lake Sharpe in South Dakota as wind gusts to 60 miles per hour roared down the reservoir, creating huge waves. Another time, the whole tournament field of 130 boats got caught in wind on Lake Erie in Ohio. That day, 15 boats swamped and many more broke their hulls and lost their trolling motors as they snapped off the transoms. Still another time, strong southeast winds created 19-foot waves at Bay de Noc in Michigan while we were competing in a championship.

Trying to slow the boat down to get an effective lure presentation in big waves and wind can be quite a challenge even to the most experienced angler. Professional anglers are more often than not, out on the water on days when the average angler opts to stay on shore. They have to catch fish. Many times their livelihood depends on it.

While there are some professional fishermen who look forward to a good wind, most would rather it be calm or only slightly breezy. They prefer to adjust their presentation to the calm conditions, rather than fight to control the boat in big swells or offshore wind shear.

Not only do wind and waves make for tough boat control, but they wreak havoc with the body as well. After a day of fighting big waves, every muscle and bone aches as a result of being tossed to and fro. On cold days, the waves crashing over the bow and the spray in the face is at best, very uncomfortable and at worst results in hypothermia. More than a few anglers I know have been taken to the hospital after a day of competition with broken bones after being slammed to the floor or against the windshield by a rogue wave.

While it might seem crazy to the average angler than anyone would fish in such conditions, if it is your job, you really have little choice. Some competitors will seek out a sheltered area and spend the day there, but if there are no fish in that area, all they have accomplished is that they stayed comfortable. Most often those who stuck their faces into the teeth of the wind and persevered against the elements come in with good catches of fish.

Of course, risking one's safety or that of your fishing partner all in the name of catching a limit or winning a tournament is foolish. There will always be another tournament. There will always be another day to fish. That's where wisdom comes in. In professional angling, as well as any other career, wisdom comes with experience. And you never gain wisdom or experience if every day is calm and sunny. In fact, it has been proven time and again that more wisdom is gained through the rough times and defeats of life than through the easy times and victories.

Just as a professional fisherman's skill is tested during times of high winds and rough seas, so can a Believer's faith be tested. During those times of testing, it is imperative that we have wisdom to persevere through the trial. The brother of Jesus put it this way in James, chapter 1: "Consider it pure joy, my brothers, whenever you face trials of many kinds, because you know that the testing of your faith develops perseverance. Perseverance must finish its work so that you may be mature and complete, not lacking anything. If any of you lacks wisdom, he should ask God, who gives generously to all without finding fault, and it will be given to him. But when he asks, he must believe and not doubt, because he who doubts is like a WAVE OF THE SEA, BLOWN AND TOSSED BY THE WIND (emphasis mine). That man should not think he will receive anything from the Lord; he is a double-minded man, unstable in all he does."

By asking God for wisdom, we are asking for a solution to a situation not from our point of view, but from HIS point of view. And scripture promises that he will give us His point of view if we only ask and then believe.

Do you feel "tossed by the wind" today, as you face a trial or problem in your family, job or relationship with the Lord? The Bible says to "trust in the Lord and lean not on your own understanding" (Proverbs 3:5). Why not ask the One who is All-Knowing for His solution, and then wait for His answer to come. Once the trial is placed in His hands, then and only then, can any of us experience the "peace that passes all understanding," that He has promised.

Chapter Thirteen

"Snake in the Boat"

Because I'm a touring professional fisherman, I often end up fishing in some interesting places. Some of these lakes are remote and pristine while others are crowded and dirty. I've fished tournaments on the Detroit River in downtown Detroit and caught walleyes out of sewer pipes. I've also fished in such places as Ouachita Lake in the Ozark Mountains, a place so beautiful that it could well be the best fishin' hole this side of Heaven.

But few lakes can match the remoteness and beauty of Fort Peck Reservoir, a massive clear-water lake in the canyon country of northeastern Montana. There is a creek arm there by the name of Snow Creek; its beauty simply takes your breath away. In this creek arm, you might see a big mule deer drinking from the lake while listening to a bull elk bugling in the pine forests surrounding the reservoir, while at the same time fighting a 10-pound walleye at the end of your line.

On another section of the lake is Rock Creek where huge rock outcroppings form sheer drop-offs, sheltering some of the biggest smallmouth bass an angler could hope for. It was in this creek arm that I found myself one warm August morning, catching one smallmouth after another, sprinkled in with a few nice walleyes.

Under the edge of the rocky cliff, swallows were busy "chittering" as they flew back and forth feeding their young. The sky was a perfect azure and the lake was mirror calm, save for the occasional splashing of fish at the end of my line. It was like being in Fishing Paradise until the scene abruptly changed.

Suddenly, the birds began to squawk in that familiar distress call that something is wrong. I looked up to see a large snake pull one of the baby birds out of a nest and slither back up to the top of the cliff. Moments later, the serpent returned for another meal. As a die-hard bird lover, I decided to save the birds by whacking at the snake with my fishing rod. In the process, however, my lure hooked into the snake and he abruptly dropped from the cliff face into my boat.

Now, I've never really had a problem with snakes. I always figure if they leave me alone, I'll leave them alone. But I don't really care for them in my boat, especially if they are five feet long. And this snake was mad! Compounding the problem was the fact that it was hooked fast to my jigging spoon and there was little hope of getting it loose. Ordinarily, I would have cut the line, but I only had a couple of these lures and they were catching fish.

I tried to pin the snake down and pull the lure out, but his hide was too tough and he had a bad habit of trying to bite me, which wasn't good since this snake was a prairie rattler and I was alone, and there were no other boats in the horizon. The standoff lasted for several minutes until I finally got fed up with the snake trying to bite me and decided to put my boat seat pedestal to use. I'll tell you what, for a critter without legs, a snake has incredible reflexes to dodge a well-swung seat pedestal. I eventually caught him across the skull with a backswing, stunning him enough to get the lure out. I then tossed the nasty critter out of the boat and he swam away to shore.

I know what you're thinking: "Boy, was that stupid to hook that snake". You're right. Just like when we as Christians invite the devil into our lives, messing and toying with his temptations until he ends up in the boat with us. Then the battle begins as we try to get him out of our lives.

The devil, "that serpent of old" as the Bible describes him, is just like the snake in the boat. My snake wasn't a danger to me until he got in the boat. The devil isn't a danger to you until you fall to his temptations. That's when you can get bit. That's when it becomes harder and harder to get rid of him.

I learned a great practical lesson that day. But I also learned a very spiritual one as well. I have never invited a snake in my boat since and have no plans to do so in the future. That's the attitude we need to take when faced with temptation.

The Bible says: "resist the devil and he will flee". That's great advice. We are all sinners saved by grace but there's going to be times when the serpent of old gets the best of us. That's the time to take the pedestal of salvation through Jesus Christ and whack that serpent upside the head.

Chapter Fourteen

"Making the Right Connection"

Professional fishermen have everything they need to help them catch more fish. All of our equipment is top of the line, state-of-the-art stuff that the recreational angler would most certainly envy. We have the best and most expensive boats, motors, trolling motors, electronics, rods, reels, nets, and lures. All of these, when combined with a lifetime on the water, enable us to catch more fish than the next guy; at least most of the time.

A well-fitted pro's fishing rig and tackle will run upwards of $70,000 and you can add another $40,000 for his tow vehicle. Yet, with all this expensive top-notch equipment, the most important tool needed to get the fish from the water to the boat is fishing line. How many times have you lost a big fish because your line broke? I know it's happened to me more than once and in my business that can get very expensive in a hurry.

Twice I can remember fish breaking my line in a tournament that ended up costing me $40,000. It hasn't happened for a long time, but it sure hurts when it does. Fishing line is one of the cheapest tools we use when fishing, yet is often taken care of the least of any of our equipment.

We use two types of line when tournament fishing; monofilament and braided. Monofilament is petroleum based and stretches somewhat, while braided line is fabric with no stretch at all. Monofilament line is sensitive to exposure to the sun and can rot quite quickly, while braided line is more heat resistant and lasts much longer. Braided line is also more abrasion resistant than monofilament.

When we choose the right lure to cast to the fish, it is our line that makes the connection to the lure. Without strong line, most fish would get away. Professionals change their monofilament at least once a week and many every other day to assure that stretch hasn't weakened the line.

Oh yeah, there is one more crucial element when fishing that probably results in more lost fish than anything else; knot strength. Bad knots will most certainly cause fish to break off. Most fishing lines today are strong, but they are only as strong as the knot you tie. Fishing pros generally use two knots: the improved clinch and the Palomar knot. Both knots have breaking strength stronger than the line test being used.

I've always considered the Bible as my fishing line to God. There is strength and power in God's Word that keeps me connected to Him so He can reel me in. And while the Bible is the line, reading it is the knot. The more I read it, the stronger my knot becomes. I look at the Bible as braided line. It isn't flexible, it doesn't stretch or change.

Prayer is another line to God and I look at it as monofilament. It can be weak like 2-pound test or strong like 30 pound-test fishing line. Prayer can be stretched, and flexible. The knot is praying all things in the name of Jesus.

Like fishing line, however, prayers not said and a Bible not read is like monofilament lying in the sun. Our connection to the Lord is weakened and in danger of breaking off.

As believers, we have more tools and equipment than any generation before us to help us live a Godly life. Yet none of those resources matter if we neglect our line to God. The Bible tells us to "cast all our cares upon Him, for He cares for you".

Do you feel disconnected from God? If so, then it's time to change your line. Re-spool your life with his Word then make a cast out to Him in prayer.

You will be amazed what you might catch.

Chapter Fifteen

"Good Fish/Bad Fish"

People often ask me if I catch any other kinds of fish besides walleyes when I'm fishing a walleye tournament. The answer, of course, is that I certainly do, often much to my chagrin. I believe that over the course of 30 years of tournament fishing, I have caught just about every species of freshwater fish that swims, at least in the lakes where we have had tournaments.

The list is long, and I may have forgotten some, but just to give you an idea that most fish will bite on the same things as walleyes, I've decided to list those that I have caught over the years: northern pike, musky, sauger, saugeye, chain pickerel, largemouth and smallmouth bass, spotted bass, white bass, striped bass, wiper, striper, channel cat, blue cat, flathead cat, bullhead, eelpout, sucker, redhorse, carp, quillback, buffalo, drum, sturgeon, whitefish, cisco, mooneye, Chinook salmon, coho salmon, steelhead, crappie, bluegill, sunfish, perch, rock bass, and probably a few others.

While all of these fish are fun to catch, they can be a big annoyance in a walleye tournament (with the exception of sauger and saugeye which often count as a walleye) because they consume a lot of time and energy when one is fishing against the clock. All these fish, of course, are quickly returned back to the water since they can't be weighed as part of the bag at the end of the day. Sometimes, I'd like to keep a few for a fish fry later on, but these fish would rob the desired tournament fish of valuable oxygen in the livewell, which could kill them. So back they go.

Jesus talks about a similar scenario in Matthew 13:47 when he says: "Once again, the kingdom of heaven is like a net that was let down into the lake and caught all kinds of fish. When it was full, the fishermen pulled it up on the shore. Then they sat down and collected the good fish in baskets, but threw the bad away. This is how it will be at the end of the age. The angels will come and separate the wicked from the righteous and throw them into the fiery furnace, where there will be weeping and gnashing of teeth."

Wow. I think I like the "Fisherman's Prayer" better: "I pray that I may live to fish until my dying day, and when it comes to my last cast, then I most humbly pray; when in the Lord's great landing net and peacefully asleep, that in his mercy, I be judged big enough to keep!"

The Bible is full of stories about the love of Christ and His compassion for people. Yet sometimes He said things that were quite unnerving. Matthew 13 is one of them. I guess if I was Christ and came to earth as a human to suffer terrible torture and give up my very life for undeserving and ungrateful people, I'd be issuing the same warning. In this chapter, Jesus is very adamant that there is a place of eternal suffering for the unbeliever, contrary to a lot of teaching in many of today's churches.

Christ's message in Matthew is clear: accept His free gift of salvation through His death on the cross and you will be judged big enough to keep!

Chapter Sixteen

"What Are You Fishing For?"

I have many friends, some of them even Christians, who spend way more time in the presence of fish than in the presence of God. The lakes, rivers and streams are their church and their excuse. They worship the creation rather than the Creator.

We do know, of course, that God is in all of his creation. Romans 1:20 states that "Since the creation of the world His invisible attributes, His eternal power and divine nature, have been clearly seen, being understood through what has been made, so they are without excuse."

I also have friends who understand the above verse while spending time in the outdoors and draw strength from being surrounded by the natural order of things that God has created. One such friend is author and Dove Award winner, Steve Chapman, whom I've been blessed to have served with more than once at evangelistic events around the country.

In his book, "Reel Time with God", Steve states that "The outdoors is one of the best places to improve the "inner man". If we take the time to "get out there," God will make Himself known in ways we never expected." Steve has written several books about the outdoors and drawing close to the Lord through nature. I've read them all. Yet he never, ever, replaces church with time in the outdoors.

In one of his chapters in "Reel Time" titled; 'Remember the Sabbath,' Steve talks about the temptation to go crappie fishing on a warm, spring Sunday morning instead of being in church. Now I don't know about you, but I sure can relate to this one! At the end of the story, Steve resists the temptation to go fishing and submits to God's perfect will.

He then ends the chapter with this prayer: *"Thank you, Father, for making the Sabbath. It is the governor of passions for people like me who love to be outside. I pray for the courage to always choose to be with my fellow believers as often as possible. You are worthy to be praised-far more than what You made. In Jesus' name, amen."*

What a terrific prayer for those of us who struggle with going hunting or fishing on Sunday morning instead of going to church. It is one worth writing out and sticking it on the visor of the pick-up truck, the console of the boat, the cover of the tackle box, and the lid of the bait bucket!

I have to say that there have been many Sunday mornings when I went out hunting or fishing, then raced home, changed clothes and headed off to church, often wishing I could just stay in the woods or on the lake. But once at the service, I was happy to be there and had no regrets about getting out of the boat, tree stand or duck blind.

It is important to God that we spend time with Him and we can do that wherever we are since he created it all. But it is likewise important that we spend time in fellowship with people of "like and precious faith," and that we "forsake not the fellowship of other believers." His Word tells us so, and that directive is accomplished best every Sunday morning at church.

In Steve's book, his final words are these: "Casting into the deep pools of God's Word, you'll discover honest insights, uplifting spiritual truths, and unabashed enthusiasm for living in Christ. As you explore God's timeless wisdom and revel in His gracious provision, you'll discover that He is the true source of life…and fish!"

I couldn't have said it better myself.

66

Chapter Seventeen

"Powerful or Powerless?"

Powerful. The dictionary describes this word as "full of or having power or influence". The opposite word, powerless, is described as "lacking power, force or energy". Power is talked about daily in most people's lives. We use power to run our cars, light, heat and cool our homes, run our country, defeat our foes, hit a home run.

As a tournament angler, I would be lost without power. Batteries start my engine, run my navigation equipment, turn on my locators, pump my bilge, fill my livewells and power my trolling motor. Once started, power gets me where I want to go with my big motor. Once fishing, power in my bow-mount electric motor keeps me on the spot in wind and current.

A few years back, I was fishing the In-Fisherman Professional Walleye Trail Championship at Wisconsin's Lake Mendota. I had a small, rocky spot in 18-29 feet of water, but did not want to anchor on it since it was what we call a "sliver" which means it was about two feet wide, but about 50 feet long. I could use the power in my electric trolling motor to position the boat over the sliver, then steer it back and forth while jigging vertically along the edge. This allowed my to constantly work the sliver from one end to the other, catching any fish that moved up to feed.

Even in a strong wind, the power of my 82-pound thrust trolling motor kept me right where I needed to be. I already had two fish in the boat early in the morning, when suddenly, I was no longer able to hold the boat on the sliver. Every time I hit the foot control that powered the motor, I would hear it kick in, but the boat was still drifting away from the spot. Something was definitely wrong.

I quickly pulled up the motor to see what the problem was, when much to my dismay, I noticed that the propeller was missing! Now usually I would have a spare in the boat, but I had just upgraded to a larger motor, so the spare prop wouldn't fit. Fortunately, I was able to radio to tournament headquarters and my good friends from the MotorGuide tech truck came out in a boat and replaced the prop. Although I lost valuable fishing time, I was still able to catch a limit that day.

I also learned a valuable lesson. Besides making sure that I always have a spare prop that fits, I learned that all the potential power, in this case an 82-pound thrust motor, moves nothing if it isn't connected to a propeller. It's kind of like having a 440 horsepower car engine that isn't hooked up to a transmission. It sounds good when it's running, but you're not going anywhere!

The Bible is often referred to as God's Word and millions of sermons have been preached over the years about its power. In Hebrews 4:12-13, the Bible proclaims "For the word of God is living and active. Sharper than any double-edged sword, it penetrates even to dividing soul and spirit, joints and marrow; it judges the thoughts and attitudes of the heart. Nothing in all creation is hidden from God's sight. Everything is uncovered and laid bare before the eyes of him to whom we must give account."

Whew! Sounds pretty powerful to me. I know that when I need to hear from God or I need something powerful to happen in my life, I can always find the solution by reading and meditating on his word. Although the answer may not always be immediate, it is always there.

Yet a closed or unread Bible is able to produce no power at all. It is like a motor with no gas. The potential is there, but it must be read and believed before its power can be unleashed. Without action on our part, the Bible becomes no more than a dust-collector, a Christian ornament to decorate our coffee table to impress our Christian friends.

Far too many Christians today try to get their spiritual power one hour on Sunday at church or watching Christian television, reading Christian books, listening to Christian tapes, attending Christian conferences. While these can be good things, they are worthless if they replace the reading of God's word.

You want power? Then read the most powerful book ever written. Opening the Book starts the engine. Reading it moves you forward. Meditating on it gives you more power to be an over-comer than you could ever imagine.

Chapter Eighteen

"Fishing for Fulfillment"

Have you ever wondered why people do what they do? Why do we have a job, a career, a profession? What is the purpose of a hobby or a sport that we enjoy? Is there more than just earning a living and paying bills and plodding through life? Of course there is. The answer to all of these questions is happiness and fulfillment.

As a tournament angler, I fish to win money. When I win money, I can pay my bills and sometimes even save a little. I can help others with that money and I can give to my church to help them pay their bills and to missionaries to help them reach others with the Gospel. That makes me happy, but is it fulfilling?

There is a big difference between happiness and fulfillment. The old saying that "money can't buy happiness" is so true. Happiness is a feeling or emotion that you feel at any given moment. It can change a moment later. Fulfillment is much different. It stays with you through both the highs and the lows.

You know what, though? Money can't buy fulfillment either. In my business I meet many wealthy people. Few are happy or fulfilled. They are often too busy to enjoy their money, too afraid of someone taking advantage of them, or too scared of losing what they worked for. They are suspicious of almost anyone and have few genuine friends.

Many seek happiness and fulfillment in a life of sin, but sin never gives anyone more than a few moments of happiness and certainly no fulfillment that is long-lasting. People who try to live a life separated from God cannot experience true happiness or fulfillment because everything they do is with the wrong motivation.

Does that mean a wealthy person can't be a Christian? Of course not. Being rich or poor has nothing to do with a relationship with God. It's all about the heart, attitude, and what motivates a person. As long as both the rich and the poor understand that it is God who takes care of them and not their own strength, then their attitudes are one and the same.

Because a portion of my income is based on where I finish in a given tournament, it is important to me to catch fish. When I win, it makes me happy, as it should, but my fulfillment isn't in winning money or finishing ahead of someone else in competition. My fulfillment comes from being a good witness to others when I have a good or bad tournament, and seeing them turn their lives over to Christ.

One of my favorite verses in the Bible is found in Matthew 17. Jesus says to Peter: "go to the lake and throw out your line. Take the first fish you catch; open its mouth and you will find a four-drachma coin. Take it and give it to them for my tax and yours." I think of this verse every time a catch a fish that I know will cash a check for me. It always reminds me that Jesus is the source of my income and success, not me or the fish.

Fishing for fulfillment means fishing for men, not for fish. We have been given a charge to be witnesses for Christ not only to the ends of the earth, but to the neighbor next door. When we do the job that Christ has called us to do, we will live a life of fulfillment and it is that fulfillment which brings us true happiness.

Chapter Nineteen

"Fishing Shouldn't Be This Hard"

Musky fishing is hard work. I know, because I often go musky fishing as a break from fishing for walleyes or bass. Muskies are never a common fish even in good musky waters, and the big ones only feed every three or four days, often consuming fish as big as five pounds or an occasional duck or muskrat. Even when one is hooked, it sometimes gets away through power runs, great leaps and head-shaking.

Musky tackle is heavy, comprised of big rods and reels with heavy pound-test line. The lures can be huge, some over a foot long. Most are cast away from the boat toward weedlines or sharp breaks and either steadily retrieved as is the case with bucktails, or erratically jerked back to boat when using glide baits or jerkbaits.

A good day of musky fishing is having a big fish follow the bait to the boat or having a strike or two occur. A real good day is actually catching a legal fish, which in many states is 36 or more inches. A great day would be catching four or more legal fish, which is a rare occurrence for most musky anglers.

The best time of the year to have a great day of musky fishing is in the fall as the water temperatures cool down and the fish are building up fat reserves for the winter. This great fishing lasts about three to four weeks beginning in early October. A few monster muskies are usually caught in the frigid waters of November, but most of those are taken using 3-pound live suckers for bait.

As a professional angler, I have had countless opportunities over the years to fish for all species of gamefish across this continent. But muskies have always been my favorite because of the satisfaction of catching one after hours, days or even weeks of hard work. As a minister of the Gospel and a fisher of men, the same can be said about certain individuals that I have shared Christ with over the years.

Some people, like bass and walleyes, are pretty easy to catch and convince them of their need for a savior and a personal relationship with Jesus Christ. Others, like a big musky, can take a lot more time to catch. Sometimes I can give what I think is the perfect Gospel presentation only to have a few "follows" and a "bite" or two, but not catch anyone. It is easy to give up on these people with the excuse that "well, they heard the message, now the ball is in their court. I did my job, now it's up to them to make a decision one way or the other".

If I felt that way about muskies, I would never catch any. You see, a musky will give itself away by following the lure or even striking at it, but not getting caught. But it shows me one thing, and that it was hungry for what I had to offer. I can return to that spot in October and more than likely catch that fish because that is the season in which it would be most likely to accept my presentation.

Friendship evangelism is no different. Some people simply aren't ready to be "caught" by Christ when they first hear the Gospel message. They might "follow" what they hear or even make a half-hearted attempt during a time of weakness to find meaning to the mess in their lives, but never fully commit to receiving Christ. Like a big musky, they might see and hear presentation after presentation, show some interest, but never really get hooked.

We can become as frustrated with these people as a fisherman does with a musky. The really good musky anglers, however, never give up. They simply work at catching that fish until they finally do even if it takes them weeks, months or years. They don't try tricks, magic baits or change their presentation. They simply persevere.

That should be our approach to those who need Christ in their lives, but simply haven't made that commitment. There will come a time, a season, when they will be hungry, like an autumn musky, for the "peace that passes all understanding" that only Jesus has to offer.

Will you or I be there to catch them?

Chapter Twenty

"Dressing the Part"

Full-time professional anglers are often filmed while on the water and sometimes even while waiting for the take-off. They are also often photographed or filmed walking to the weigh-in stage or coming off the stage. Interviews can take place on and off the water during a day of competition. Therefore, it is important that they always dress the part.

Sponsor logos and images don't appear by accident when you see pro anglers on television or their image in a newspaper or magazine. Crafty veterans know how important it is to have strategically-place logos on their clothing at all times just in case the camera is rolling.

We also dress the part when it comes to inclement weather. Waterproof raingear, rubber boots and warm gloves are essential to keep us from getting cold or even getting hypothermia when fishing the early spring events. While this might sound like common sense, quite often pros, especially the young ones, will head out on the lake underdressed. The numbing cold that follows can easily affect their fishing performance.

Finally, and most importantly, we always wear our life vests while our outboard motor is running. Accidents can happen and a vest can be a life saver. We even wear them at times while fishing on rough days, not only to keep us afloat if a rogue wave should knock us overboard, but the tight-fitting vest helps to hold in heat.

While wearing clothing with the right logos help us to promote sponsors at any time, the extreme weather gear and vest can be essential to protect us and maybe even save us, should tragedy strike while on the water.

How about you? As a Christian, are you dressing the part? Do you wear clothing that promotes your number one sponsor, Jesus Christ, or do you wear clothes that might be embarrassing to Him? I'm not saying that you have to wear a T-shirt with all the right "Christianese" written on it; unless of course, you want to. What I am saying is that I sometimes see Christian outdoorsmen with some pretty offensive hunting and fishing shirts that certainly don't give glory to God and are a poor witness to their non-believing friends.

More important, however, is the question: are you wearing your Christian "life vest"?
Ephesians 6:13 says: "Therefore put on the full armor of God, so that when the day of evil comes, you may be able to stand your ground, and after you have done everything, to stand." God has given us a life vest (Eph: 14-18) to save us from a "day of evil" much as a life vest can keep an angler who goes overboard afloat long enough for rescue.

Just as a tournament director exhorts the anglers to wear the life vests throughout the day, so the Bible also exhorts Christians to "put on the full armor of God" everyday, not just in case the "day of evil" comes. You notice that the verse says WHEN the day of evil comes, not IF!

Therefore it is important that we take the full armor that God has given us, and dress in it daily. To not do so would be like fishing in shorts and t-shirts when it's snowing or even worse, to put on everything to keep us warm, but not wear our life vest. You notice that it says "the FULL armor of God" not just some of the armor of God. Sadly, too many Christians go into their day dressed in only part of their armor. Not a good idea when we have our daily battles to fight.

More than ever, I think the times we live in dictate the importance of Ephesians 6:13 to all Christians.

Are YOU dressing the part?

Chapter Twenty One

"Raising an Awareness"

Have you ever noticed how some people are unaware of what's going on around them? I don't know about you, but I see this all of the time when engaging in casual conversation about the outdoors, whether it be about hunting, fishing, birding or what have you.

Local, state and federal agencies are sometimes painfully aware of this phenomenon regarding their constituents, as are service groups, self-help groups and of course, church groups and community outreaches. The question from these groups is almost always the same: "doesn't anyone out there know what we are doing and what problems we are facing?

Many of these organizations have responded to this question by creating public relations programs to help people understand why they exist and what they are doing in the public interest. The best at this is the many conservation groups such as Ducks Unlimited, the Wild Turkey Federation, Pheasants Forever, Walleyes for Tomorrow, the Nature Conservancy and Trout Unlimited just to name a few.

These groups continuously put their need before the general public and have been very successful in raising funds to make substantial and long-lasting projects come to fruition. Many of our state and local agencies are doing the same. They have learned that when people are aware of a problem or need, they are much more willing to respond.

We often hear about the new "environmental awareness" among people of the outdoors, including companies, consumers and non-consumptive users of our natural resources. Raising the environmental awareness has long been a buzzword phrase for outdoor agencies.

I believe that the church should be doing the same thing. That is, raising the "God awareness" in their communities. Outdoor ministries such as God's Great Outdoors has been involved in doing this for many years. Some churches have responded enthusiastically to these outreaches. Many have not.

Over the years, I have spoken in more than 100 different churches at game feeds, sportsman's dinners, father and son, father and daughter, and other events with the sole purpose of raising a God-awareness in the men, women and children of the area. And it works.

Too many churches gauge the "success" of an event on the immediate response of people attending the event or declared salvations at the end of the speaker's presentation. While these things are good and one of the reasons for doing an outreach event, it is important not to forget the long-term affect that holding and advertising such events has on the community.

In our church, we have had people attend these events for years before finally coming to church and we have had people that have resisted attending the event because it was church sponsored that finally come because all of their friends are going. While not everyone gets saved (even Jesus couldn't convince everyone to follow Him), there is an awareness of God that takes place in people's lives; people who would never darken the doors of a church.

During the early days of the Christian church, the apostles and their disciples preached throughout the Holy Land to both Jews and Gentiles. Many were added to the Kingdom on a daily basis, but not everyone made a decision to follow Christ at that moment. No doubt many came along later as they saw the life-changing power of Jesus Christ manifested in their relatives and friends.

There are lots of ways churches can raise a God-awareness in their community besides doing outdoor ministry, however, I choose to do outdoor ministry because that is where God has placed me to fulfill his command to reach the lost and to exercise the "ministry of reconciliation" that He has give to ALL Christians, not just the pastors.

It is time for the Christian church to begin to raise a "God-awareness" in their community. We have been "doing church" for way too long, while those living right next door have been dying and going into a Godless eternity because no one told them about salvation through Jesus Christ.

God is at work all around us. Let's get out there and tell folks what He is doing!

Chapter Twenty Two

"Winning the Big One!"

As a professional fisherman and Super Pro Champion, it's been interesting to observe the various strategies employed by contestants over the years seeking to win the big prize.

On one hand, WHO YOU KNOW can make a big difference, especially if that person guides on the lake or is familiar with the best spots and techniques. Of course, you have to place total trust in that person and that's not easy to do with anyone nowadays.

On the other hand, relying totally on YOURSELF by working hard and studying the water before the event but not consulting with anyone else, is a strategy some anglers will use, but most often with limited or no success.

Others will rely totally on what they call LUCK for their success (not a good idea) while still others will drive their boats frantically from place to place in a NEVER-ENDING SEARCH for the right spot.

At the end of the tournament day, the WEIGHMASTER will tally the weights of each contestant's fish. His decision is final. There will only be one WINNER.

Our life here on earth can be a lot like a fishing tournament. In the Tournament of Life, people will seek many ways to win the prize, which is Heaven. And just like in a fishing tournament, most of these ways will fail.

Some will rely on LUCK ("if I'm lucky enough, God will show mercy on me and let me in at the last minute").

Still others will depend on THEMSELVES, hoping that enough prayers, good works, going to church or their religion will be enough. Finally, some will go on a NEVER-ENDING SEARCH to find their own "spirituality".

Yet none of these techniques will win the Tournament of Life!

There is only one way to win the Tournament of Life and that is WHO YOU KNOW. He is the ultimate Guide and can be totally trusted. His name is Jesus Christ. In the Bible, Jesus said: "I am the way, the truth and the life, no man comes to the Father but by me." (John 14:6). Quite simply, if you do not know Jesus, it is impossible to win the Tournament of Life.

Know Jesus? How can anyone really know Jesus? It's quite simple, really. In fact, it's so easy that many religions have found ways to make it complicated through rituals and doctrines so that sinners (you, me, everyone on earth) would have to rely on THEM to help us get to Heaven. But Jesus said that being religious isn't enough to get any of us into Heaven (John 3:3).

Fortunately for all of us, God made it simple so that all can be saved. Here's all you have to do: Call upon Jesus to forgive your sins. Tell Him you will trust Him to run your life. Ask Him to be your Friend. Acknowledge that he died for YOU, personally. Ask Him to come into your heart and into your life.

Wouldn't it be great to know ahead of time that you were going to win a tournament prize? Well, here's what God's Word, the Bible, says about winning the Tournament of Life: "I write these things to you who believe in the name of the Son of God so that you may KNOW that you have eternal life". (1 John 5:13).

The other great news is that unlike a fishing tournament, which has only one winner, the Tournament of Life will have many winners. In the Bible, God weighed a king and his kingdom and found them wanting. As a result, they lost the Tournament of Life.

For all of us, the Tournament of Life will someday come to an end. It could be today, tomorrow, next week or next year. Only God knows for certain. But on that day, we will be weighed in the balances by God the WEIGHMASTER. If we are found wanting, the Bible says we will be "cast into the Lake of Fire", losers of the Tournament of Life for all eternity.

However, the good news is if we know His Son, Jesus Christ as our personal Savior,   we will all be WINNERS.

God Himself has guaranteed it!

Chapter Twenty Three

"Get Out in the River"

Have you ever fly fished for cutthroat trout? I have, and there is something almost spiritual about casting a fly in the cold waters of the Yellowstone River with the snow-crested Rocky Mountains looming in the background. All around you are elk, bison, mule deer and an occasional grizzly bear. Oh yes, and people.

Folks by the thousands flock to Yellowstone National Park to fish the famous river every summer and enjoy the wildlife, erupting geysers and some of the most spectacular and beautiful scenery on earth. But my attraction to this special place was, and always will be, the big, golden cutthroat trout that make the Yellowstone River their home.

The first time I fished there, I was surprised and somewhat dismayed by the number of anglers lining the riverbank. Some would wade out into the frigid waters to get away from the crowd, but usually not too far from shore as the water is swift and the rocks underfoot are slippery. One slip and an angler's fishing could be ruined for the day.

In my role as a seminar and motivational speaker, I work with crowds all of the time, but when it comes to fishing, I prefer to have a place all to myself. That is why I rarely fish around "boat packs" in tournaments and will often drive past a parking lot on a local trout stream if there is another car parked there.

When I'm fishing for fun, I enjoy the solace that being alone with nature can offer. So when I saw the crowds at Yellowstone's Fishing Bridge, I decided to don my chest waders and head downstream away from everyone. Trout were rising to an insect hatch all over the river that day, but it seemed the larger fish were further out from shore in the deeper pools.

As I cast my fly into the swirling water, I kept seeing a particularly big trout rising every minute or so where the current was broken by a huge boulder. However, it was way out in the middle of the river, and the walk out there would be treacherous with the fast-flowing current and algae-covered rocks. But I decided to take the risk.

It took quite some time to work my way to the big rock, gingerly placing my feet on the greasy bottom one step at a time. Twice, I had to go around water that was too deep for my waders, but I finally made it. With the first cast of the fly, I had my prize; a prettier-than-words-can-describe cutthroat trout.

Because I was alone, there were no pictures taken, but that fish is burned in my memory forever. As I released it back behind the boulder, I thought of how my grandfather, a lifelong fly fisherman, would have loved to have had that experience. He had never gotten to fish this river, but it was his fly rod I used that day to catch my first cutthroat. Before the day was done, I would catch many more.

If I had stayed on the bank or in the shallow water that day, I may or may not have caught those trout. And while wading out to the middle of the river across slippery rocks and through deep water was risky, the rewards were worth it.

I feel the same way about my spiritual life. While it might be more comfortable to stand on the riverbank and only occasionally wade out into the shallows, how can one really experience the deep things of God? Bank-sitters will always stay dry, but quite often so is their relationship with the Lord. And while some may test the shallow water, they turn back at the slightest slip, for fear of real commitment to the goal. So while their relationship with God may not by dry, it will be as shallow or deep as the water they retreated from.

What is the goal? To be more Christ-like. Way too many people are content with being dry or shallow in their relationship with Christ. Those who want a closer relationship with Him will leave the comfort of the bank or shallows and seek the deeper love that He has to offer. That is the best catch of all.

Are you ready and willing to experience the deeper things of God today? Then let's go wading!

Chapter Twenty Four

"Cast Adrift"

Drifting: it is one of the most timeless methods for catching fish. Before outboard motors were invented, drifting with the wind or the current while dragging a line through the water was the only way to cover lots of area of a river or lake during a day of fishing. The only other way was to paddle or row-troll around the lake.

Believe it or not, many of today's modern professional anglers rely on drifting from time to time to present their lures to the fish. When the wind is right, it can be a great way to catch lots of fish. Drifting down a river and vertical jigging along the current break is also a popular method of fishing, especially for walleyes.

The drawback, however, is that while drifting, the angler's lure isn't always where the fish are. Sometimes you can drift for a mile without a bite, simply because the fish are in a different zone or perhaps in shallower or deeper water than the boat. Also, the wind or current might be moving the boat too fast for a decent lure presentation which would prevent the fish from taking the bait.

Professional anglers often compensate by adjusting their boat position by moving forward or back with their motor. To combat heavy wind, the may use a drift sock, which is similar to a wind sock, but collects large volumes of water when placed over the side, thus slowing the boat down. With these two methods, they can stay on a tight break-line or at a precise depth. It is what is referred to in fishing lingo as a "controlled drift".

Over the years, I have personally had great success with this method of fishing, but have always had to rely on some kind of auxiliary power to keep the boat in position, even if it was a paddle, oars, or the rudder of a small skiff. Without the additional help, the wind or current would simply take the boat wherever it goes. It would be a vessel completely out of control.

On a big lake, it could blow you across the lake, making for a long paddle back. On a river, the consequences could be much worse, as the current could take you over a rapids or dam. Drifting into danger on a river can be very deceiving as anyone who canoes knows that the current slows down right before a dam or rapids.

The same holds true in our Christian lives. There are many out there today who are adrift in their relationship with God. They've allowed the winds of apathy or the currents of daily struggles to take them adrift with no rudder and no power. They have decided that it is much easier to drift than to paddle hard against the current of temptation and the winds of sin.

Some have drifted so far they can no longer see the shore or find hope in ever getting back. Some have drifted to the very precipice of a waterfall or rapids and see no hope of escape.

But I have good news. There is hope and there is power. It is in God's Holy Word. Nothing can steer the boat straighter than diving into the Word when all seems hopeless and lost. The first step is to stop the drifting. The Word of God is an anchor that will stop the boat. Once the drifting has stopped, you can begin to have the hope that all is not lost. With hope comes clear thinking once again and the desire to get back on the right course.

Don't allow your life to become shipwrecked because you've drifted away from God. And don't fool yourself into believing that you have your drifting under control (controlled drift) and that you can move back and forth from a spiritual life to a non-spiritual life at will. The deception here is that YOU are controlling the boat and not God. When that happens, you're never going to steer the boat as straight as it needs to be.

It is so good to know that the Lord is our anchor when we need to stop what we are doing. And then He becomes the rudder of our lifeboat to steer us back into a right relationship with Him.

Chapter Twenty Five

"Been Fishin' Lately?"

It seems like everywhere I go, people seem to open our conversation with: "Have ya been fishin'?" Whether I'm in the restaurant, the bait shop, a trade show or even church, I get asked that question more than I care to hear it. I guess that's what one should expect, being a professional fisherman. It seems that most folks think that all I do is fish everyday. Of course, if that's all I did, I wouldn't get much else done.

The truth of the matter is that most of my fishing time is spent during tournament competition and that I don't often fish while I'm home in between events. When I do go, I prefer the quietness of a trout stream or perhaps fly fishing for panfish. I will go ice fishing in the winter in between speaking engagements and trade shows. I love to fish for muskies each fall, if I can squeeze in a trip, but that's about it.

Because tournaments can be so demanding of time, consuming 10 days straight per event and two weekends, I prefer to spend my time away from the tournament trail visiting my family. Yet, there are times when I will grab the old fishing rod and go fishing just for fun. Sometimes, when I'm feeling a little "down", being alone on the lake or stream with just me and the fish is good therapy. I kind of know how Peter felt after Jesus was crucified, when he told his friends "I go a-fishing."

Being on the road a lot in winter, I listen to tapes and spend many hours in contemplation about my profession and ministry. On a recent trip home from Minneapolis, I was driving and praying and thinking about an upcoming speaking event at a church, when the Lord spoke these words to my spirit: "Been fishin' lately?"

Mark 1:17 says, "Come, follow me" Jesus said, "and I will make you fishers of men." I began to think about all the stuff I do at my church: serving on the board, teaching Bible study, maintenance stuff, meetings with my pastor, attending Sunday service and other church events, etc. It seemed that God was trying to tell me that maybe I was spending more time polishing my boat, talking about fishing, reading about fishing instead of actually fishing!

Not that all of the things we do for our church family aren't important. They are. But sometimes we can get so caught up in working for God that we forget what he has called us to do. It's kind of like when I spend lots of days in a row on the water at tournaments, I just don't feel like fishing on my days off. In the same way, after spending days and days working for the church, when we get a break are we still reaching those who don't know Christ and His promise of salvation, or is our non-church time consumed with recreation, work and family?

Jesus has called every Christian to be a "fisher of men". Reaching the lost men and women of this world is not and never has been optional.

What would your answer be if Jesus were to say to you: "been fishin' lately?"

Chapter Twenty Six

"Losing Your Power"

Tournament fishermen are constantly talking about power. We all have big motors that power our boat, smaller motors for "power trolling" and electric motors on the bow and stern for "position fishing". All of our motors have specialty propellers that maximize the efficiency of the power generated by either gasoline or 36-volt batteries. Power is everything when it comes to tournament fishing.

Whenever a competitor has a bad day on the tournament circuit, the excuse is often due to a power failure. Sometimes they blow a powerhead that runs their big engine, or drain down the starting battery so low there isn't enough power to start the motor. Other times, trolling motor batteries can be drained half way through the day because of strong winds or current which force the fisherman to run his motor at a higher rate of speed to keep his boat in position.

I remember just such a situation at a tournament in South Dakota when the winds were blowing 25 miles per hour at the start of the day. Early on, I had no trouble controlling the boat, but by noon, the winds were gusting to over 50 miles per hour and my trolling motor batteries were down to nothing. Other guys were having the same problem and many of them opted to leave the spot and find calmer waters to fish. Unfortunately, there often are no fish in the calm waters.

I tried to hold the boat with my smaller, gas motor, but the winds were so fierce that it just wouldn't work. I then tried to anchor on a good spot but again, the wind and current simply dragged the anchor across the bottom, no matter how much rope I let out. I finally solved the problem by backing into the wind with my 200 horse power main motor. It worked fine, except for the waves splashing over the boat's transom and into the boat.

Adding to the misery was a steady dose of sleet and rain, coming down sideways with the northwest winds. I watched other boats spinning wildly out of control in the swirling winds but with my bilge pump running full time and one hand on the steering wheel and the other on my fishing rod, I was still able to hold the boat over a small spot and finally catch the last two fish I needed for a limit and a top money finish in the event.

Sometimes as believers, we can go into a week feeling full of God's power, only to be confronted by the winds and storms of life. Suddenly, our spiritual batteries become drained and we are buffeted and tossed to and fro, out of control, until emotions take over and just like a fisherman, try to find shelter from the storm.

We know that Jesus is a storm-calmer in our lives, but there are also times He wants us to face the challenge to grow us in our faith. I know this isn't what Christians want to hear, but it is a reality which we must face from time to time in our lives. It is what makes us strong and makes us victorious.

Christians have three sources of power to face the storms of life, just as anglers have three sources of power for boat control. These are prayer, the power of the Spirit and the Word of God. When we don't pray or read the Bible, our spiritual batteries can become drained in a hurry. When a storm hits, those batteries can go dead in short order. Suddenly, we feel powerless over our situation. The good news is that we still have a reserve source of power and that is the Holy Spirit. It is He who gives us the power we need in a time of weakness to overcome the storm.

How many times have we faced trials and felt like giving up or just seeking to get away from the storm? I know that I've been there more times than I care to remember. But God says, "Whoa, back up! I will never leave you nor forsake you. I will give you the power to overcome this adversity in your life!" Often, we simply must rely on the power of the Spirit to carry us through and not give up.

After a day on the water when my batteries go dead, I have to hook them up on a charger so I can fish the next day. We must do the same thing in our spiritual lives to overcome the temptations and storms thrown at us each day. Living all week on the spiritual charge of a Sunday service isn't going to cut it.

The Bible tells us to be "filled *daily* with the Spirit". If we follow that advice, we will be given the power to overcome anything that comes our way.

Chapter Twenty Seven

"The New Breakthrough"

American consumers are always looking for something new to help them to succeed. Fishermen are no different. In my 30 years of professional fishing, I feel like I've pretty much seen it all. Yet, as the years go by, someone always seems to come up with a new lure or new technique that is "banned in six countries" because it catches too many fish.

Fishermen are just as gullible as the fish they chase. If you don't believe me, just check out one of the hundreds of outdoor "super stores" spread across the country. These fishing malls are jam-packed with wall after wall of new products every winter. Fishing pros from across the country come in during "fishing extravaganza days" and help the store to promote the latest and greatest lure that will make anyone a better fisherman.

Billions of dollars are spent on these new baits as well as the new equipment needed to fish a new presentation concocted by marketing people who seldom step into a boat or ever cast a line into the water. The buyer can't wait until the warm winds of spring melt the ice so that he or she can test out their newfound technique with their new and innovative lure. Outdoor magazine headlines leap out at you with the words NEWEST BREAKTHROUGH! Whatever.

These "fishing fads" as we professionals like to call them, catch fire for a year or two before fizzling out. The lures end up in a close-out shopping cart jammed with several other brands of the latest and the greatest. Those that were bought eventually find their way into some kids' tackle box, as Dad needs to make room for the next new thing.

Smart anglers realize that the new technique might have caught some fish, but it seems they caught a lot more fishing the old, tried and true methods that have been taught and refined by fishing experts for many decades.

The Church has been called to become fishers of men. Like many fishers of fish, it always seems to be looking for a new lure or new technique to accomplish this command. Today, there are more books, magazines, tv shows and even networks that teach and preach on how to be a better Christian and how to lead others to Christ.

It seems that you can't turn on Christian television anymore without someone screaming and hollering about a "new revelation" (which the Bible calls "every wind of doctrine"). Of course, the teaching and revelation is always accompanied by the speaker's latest book, video or teaching series. Studies show that Christians spend way more time reading Christian books than they do the Bible. Interesting.

There are probably few Christians who haven't received a "prayer cloth" or rug in the mail, or a vial of sand from the Israeli desert, a hunk of gopher wood or some other Christian "good luck charm". And of course, there is the flood of e-mail messages that if you send them on to at least 10 people God will bless you. Of course if you DON'T send them, you really don't love Jesus. Give me a break!

Just as fishermen would be much better off studying and perfecting the few techniques that actually work to catch fish on a consistent basis, so should the Christian quit messing around with all the new stuff, blow the dust off the Bible and not just read it, but *study* the Word of God.

Christians need to quit substituting tv preachers for fellowship with the body of Christ in a local church. They need to stop reading and believing every new revelation that comes along and start reading and believing the inspired Word of God. They need to quit playing the "spiritual lottery" by doing good works to please God with the hope of balancing it all out against the willful sin in their lives.

People often seem amazed as to why the American church is so weak in its faith. Ask the average Christian how many hours a week they pray or read their Bible and they think you are from Mars. Most Believers read their Bible once a week, if at all, and few pray more than five minutes a day counting the blessing at mealtime. Fewer and fewer Christians can be seen carrying their Bibles into church because scripture is now presented to them on the power point. Newer Christians can't even find the book of Genesis.

If you spent this little amount of time in any other relationship, it would fail miserably. So how can any of us expect a vibrant, real and loving relationship with our Creator when we know so little about Him and talk to Him less than five minutes a day. Try that with the loved ones closest to you and see how fast those relationships go down the tubes.

God desires a loving relationship with His children. He has done His part, it's time for all of us to do ours. It's time to get back to the basic disciplines of Bible reading and prayer. Otherwise we will simply become people tossed to and fro by every wind of doctrine and every new feel-good Christian message that comes along.

Chapter Twenty Eight

"Why Great Fish?"

As an author and speaker, I come in contact with thousands of people every year both in the fishing arena and in the Christian church. Invariably, I am asked why my websites, professional business and ministry all have "Great Fish" in their titles. The answer to this question often provokes some interesting conversations, especially among those who wish they had never asked. But it also opens many doors and plants some great seeds in the heads and hearts of those who are pre-Christians.

To answer this question, I always refer to the Book of Jonah 1:17. "But the Lord provided a great fish to swallow Jonah". You see, like Jonah, I was running as far away from God as I thought possible, even though our reasons differed. For Jonah, he did not want to see the hated Assyrians, who lived in Nineveh, spared from God's wrath. For me, it was a simple matter of running from the purpose God had for my life.

You see, as God placed Jonah in a great fish not only to spare his life, but to give him time to reflect on his disobedience, so He also placed me in a great fish for the same reasons. True, I wasn't literally in the belly of a fish like Jonah, but where I was living was just as dark and stinky. For Jonah, it took three days before he overcame his stubbornness, repenting of his sin and asking God for deliverance. For me, it was almost 30 years.

But that is far from being the end of the story. Although Jonah was a significant prophet and called of God, and although it took him three days in the belly of a great fish to get an attitude adjustment, his new attitude didn't last long. Jonah obeyed God and proclaimed His impending judgment on Nineveh, only to see the people repent and be forgiven by God. Jonah's response to God's grace to the Ninevites was one of great anger (Jonah 4:1).

So Jonah went out of the city and sulked under a little shelter he had made. God provided a fast-growing vine to give him shade for a day, but then took it away, making Jonah even madder, telling the Lord that "I am angry enough to die". It is obvious that Jonah cared more about his own comfort than the lost souls of Nineveh. Have you ever been in Jonah's shoes? I know I have. Sometimes it's more comfortable not to tell people about God. Worse yet, sometimes we can become so disgusted with some people or people groups, that we have no desire or will to see them saved!

But I love God's response in Jonah 4:10. "You have been concerned about this vine, though you did not tend it or make it grow. It sprang up overnight and died overnight. But Nineveh has more than a hundred and twenty thousand people who cannot tell their right hand from their left, and many cattle as well. Should I not be concerned about that great city?"

Like Jonah, I understood God's salvation and deliverance from the belly of the great fish. But also like Jonah, I had a lot to learn about God's grace. How many of us have had or still have some "Ninevites" in our lives? They may be people who look different, think different, act different, believe different and ARE different. But God sent Christ to die for the sins of ALL mankind, not just people who make us comfortable.

Until we understand that it is the "will of the Father that none should perish but that all should come to repentance", and that it is our job, as believers, to reconcile the lost to Christ (2Co.5:18), we will be in disobedience to God and following through on the call He has for our lives.

"Standing on the Rock"

It seems like only yesterday that I caught my first walleye, but in fact, it was almost 50 years ago. Yet, I remember every detail of it. I was only five years old at the time and having been born and raised in an old, Midwestern river town, it was only natural that I should be fishing with my dad that day. My father was a fly fisherman and he was drifting a streamer fly in the current of the main river channel, catching walleyes, while I was bobber fishing for panfish in a calm, backwater slough. Although I was catching fish, I wanted to get out by Dad and catch some of those big walleyes. The problem was that in order to get out there, I would have to wade across the gravel bar and that was forbidden.

I soon lost interest in the panfish and began turning over rocks, trying to catch crayfish while in the process getting wet, muddy and stinky from river's mucky bottom. I remember crying out to my dad to let me come out by him. He finally relented and picked up his muddy, little boy and sat me on a big granite rock next to him by the river's edge.

He handed me his pole and within minutes I had caught the first walleye of my life.

Today, I am one of the top money winners on the In-Fisherman Professional Walleye Trail, the Walleye Super Pro Champion, and a full-time professional fisherman, author and speaker. One could say that my life has a fairy tale ending from a fairy tale beginning and it would be hard to argue. Yet, like most fairy tales that start out peaceful and end up perfect, the middle is always filled with villains, goblins and evil. That would pretty much describe my life.

Like most guys growing up in a small, rural town, I spent most of my early years hunting, fishing and trapping. After a two-year stint in the Army in the late 60's, I returned to my roots, got married, bought a house and settled into the routine of working, fishing and hunting, not necessarily in that order. I had 10 jobs in 10 years, mainly because I didn't like working for anyone. Socializing meant heading to the tavern after work and staying there until it closed at 2:00 a.m.

Bass tournaments were starting up at the time and I dreamed of one day becoming a pro fisherman. But it was expensive and I had a wife and five kids, couldn't keep a job and spent too much money "socializing". I knew that I had the talent to catch fish, but the villains of alcohol and poverty left me with low self-esteem and little hope for the future.

But things were about to change.

Against my family's protests, I bought a fishing boat and began guiding, fishing tournaments and doing some outdoor writing. After six years, I had built a successful guide business, won several bass tournaments and published more than 500 articles on hunting and fishing. The following season, against most people's good judgment, I quit it all to become a full-time professional walleye tournament angler. Little did I know how much that decision would change my life.

The year was 1988 and I was 39 years old. I won two tournaments that year, made more money than I had ever made before, did commercials on national television, was asked to write a book on fishing, secured sponsorships for the following year and was flying high as a kite. Yet, when autumn came and the season was over, the goblins of discouragement and depression came knocking at my door. I was drinking more than ever and I had a hole in my heart that you could drive a bass boat through. I couldn't understand why.

During the tournament season, I met Mark Dorn who worked for In-Fisherman and was the previous year's Angler of the Year. I had a lot of respect for Mark even though he was always asking me to come to the Fellowship of Christian Anglers Society meetings that were held at each tournament. Believe you me, I wanted nothing to do with religion. I considered most religious people to be hypocrites. Besides, the lake was my church and I loved and worshipped nature as my god, so I felt no need be ruled by a God who was just waiting for me to mess up (which was constantly) so he could send me to hell.

But Mark was persistent and invited me to a retreat which would be attended by Al and Ron Lindner, who were fishing heroes of mine. Thinking it would be good for my career, I accepted. The first thing I learned from the speaker that night was that God was not waiting to send me to hell, but that he loved me so much that he sent is only Son to die for my mistakes (John 3:16). The second thing I learned was that all I had to do to get right with God was to accept in my heart what the Son had done for me and I would have eternal life (Romans 10:9).

The only question I had was how could a holy God accept a dirty sinner like me? I had spent most of my life denying His existence, living my life as I wanted, worshipping the creation instead of the Creator and breaking His commandments at every turn. But I then heard that while we were yet sinners, Christ died for us. There were more than 100 men there that night, but when the speaker asked those who wanted to receive God's free gift of salvation to stand up, I was the first out of my seat.

Just like my earthly dad picked up his grubby, dirty son and sat him on the rock by the river so many years ago, God picked me up out of the dirt and grime of a sinful, hopeless life, cleaned me up and set me on the Rock of Christ. He took away the drinking, the depression, and despair and gave me a new attitude, a new life. Jesus said that He came to give us abundant life and that is what I have in Him today.

You can to by praying this simple prayer:

"Lord Jesus: Thank you for giving up your life so that I might have eternal life. Forgive me of my sins as I confess them with a repentant heart. Come into my heart and life and make me new. I receive you now, in Your Name. Amen"